Table of Contents

Executive Summary

Children aged under 18 make up nearly a quarter of the population, but because of their immaturity they have no formal voice in matters concerning their well-being. They are seen but not heard. The primary responsibility for their welfare rests with parents. Help is provided by the NHS (through GPs and community child health services), by local government (through social services and education) and by others such as voluntary agencies. This help takes many forms, and includes services available to everyone, such as immunisation against disease and child health surveillance, which involves checks (of sight and hearing, for example) to ensure that children are developing normally. It also includes more selective support when necessary, and, in extreme circumstances, it may involve protecting children from abuse and neglect. The Children Act 1989 (Ref. 1) and the new contract between GPs and the NHS (Ref. 2) have increased the responsibilities of social services authorities and GPs for safeguarding the health and development of children – traditional areas of work for community child health and education authorities. In addition, legislation (Refs. 2 and 3) emphasises that people's health and social care needs must be identified and services provided specifically to meet them. This is different from offering a fairly standard range of services and slotting people into them.

This changing approach provides a major challenge for all involved. Health and social services authorities must take three important steps if the new responsibilities are to be met, and effective services provided for children and their families without shortfalls,

duplication, or waste. Many authorities recognise the need for these steps and are seeking to take them.

— At the strategic level, agencies must assess the overall needs of children and families in their area, plan to meet those that have been agreed as priorities, and redistribute resources where necessary. At the individual level, services should be targeted to meet specific needs. In particular, the needs of children with a disability and their families should be given a higher priority. At present the services provided are often unfocused and unrelated to needs; and the reasons for providing some services are often unclear.

— Authorities should develop ways of checking whether services provided to children and families are effective. At present some £2 billion a year is spent on services provided by community child health and social services authorities, but little is known of their impact.

— Authorities and professionals must work together to plan and deliver services. Family support should be provided jointly and given a higher priority. It should make the most of the different skills of people working in health and voluntary agencies, social services and education authorities, and parents working as volunteers in the community. At present there is little joint agreement on needs and service planning; and there is ambiguity between the roles of some professionals. With responsibility for services increasingly shared between agencies, and the provision of services increasingly fragmenting, the likelihood of gaps and duplication will grow unless effective joint action is taken.

The Government could raise the status of joint children's service plans by making them mandatory between social services, health and education authorities, and requiring them to be published.

Introduction

1. The prime responsibility for the well-being of children rests with parents, but the NHS and local government have responsibilities to ensure additional support is provided in many ways. Among these are **universal services** available to all – such as immunisation, and health surveillance to check that children are developing normally. These services are in addition to treatment for children when they are sick (which is not the subject of this report). **Selective support** may be arranged for families who need more help (Exhibit 1); and in exceptional circumstances, children may become seriously neglected or abused, and be in need of **child protection**. If children's families can no longer look after them or provide them with adequate care, they may need to be **looked after** in foster homes or residential care.

2. The likelihood of families needing extra assistance increases where they live in poor housing, a poor environment, or if they suffer from ill health, anxiety, stress, unemployment or have a low income (Refs. 4 and 5). These problems can affect children in various ways. They may become physically, emotionally, mentally or socially underdeveloped through lack of adequate care. As they grow, their development or behaviour may cause concern unless their problems are addressed. They may become disturbed or delinquent. Poor housing and a poor environment

may also increase the risk of ill health and accidents (Ref. 6).

3. **Children with a disability** have particular needs. Some 3% of children are born with a disability or are injured in childhood (Ref. 7). They and their families need help, both to alleviate the degree of handicap and to cope with the extra strains imposed by caring for a disabled child.

4. The way in which the state provides support has been extensively altered by recent legislation and changes to GPs' contracts. The **NHS and Community Care Act 1990** has separated the commissioning of services from

Exhibit 1
FAMILY SUPPORT
Selective support may be arranged for families who need more help

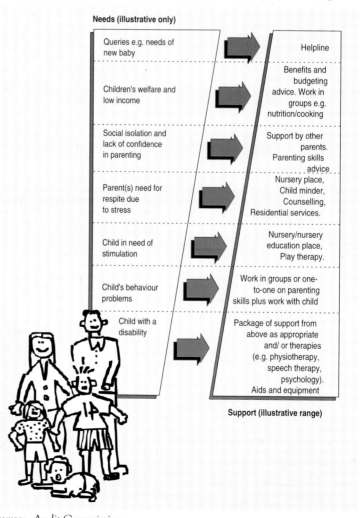

Source: *Audit Commission*

their provision, particularly in the health service, changing the emphasis from the provision of services to the meeting of needs. The **Children Act 1989** has consolidated much previous child care legislation, rebalancing the relationship between families and the state. In particular, it has introduced a new responsibility for social services authorities to identify children in need and provide pro-active support. Children in need are defined as those with disabilities and those whose health and development are at risk unless services are provided. The Act empowers social services to ask other agencies to help provide these services, although, unlike community care, jointly produced plans for children's services are recommended rather than required. Within the NHS, the **1990 GP contract** has introduced additional incentives for GPs to become more involved with health promotion, child health surveillance, and the immunisation of children – also the province of the community child health services; and the introduction of GP fund-holding has meant that some community child health services are commissioned directly by GPs rather than by district health authorities.

5. All of these changes increase the overlap of responsibilities between social services, health and education authorities and require major adjustments to the way agencies work and relate to each other. Traditionally, the health service has provided services available to everyone, while local authority social services have provided support that is more highly focused on children in particular circumstances. Although this broad distinction remains, in future, health agencies will need to focus more of their scarce

resources, while local authorities will need to broaden their remit to promote a wider range of initiatives that provide families with support. Many activities fall within the remit of both the NHS and local authorities (Exhibit 2); and even those exclusive to the NHS are shared between GPs and community child health services. The potential for duplication, confusion and waste is considerable unless these changes are managed effectively.

6. Taken together, services for safeguarding the welfare of children cost approximately £2 billion a year in England and Wales, of which three quarters is spent by local authorities (Exhibit 3, overleaf). Community child health services cost approximately £295 million, and payments to GPs account for a further £85 million.

7. Since the introduction of the 1990 GP contract, increasing numbers of GPs have taken over responsibility for immunisations and the basic programme of child health surveillance. In some family health services authorities (FHSAs), over 90% of GPs are now 'accredited' to carry out health

Exhibit 2
SERVICES PROVIDED BY THE NHS AND SOCIAL SERVICES
Many activities fall within the remit of both the NHS and social services

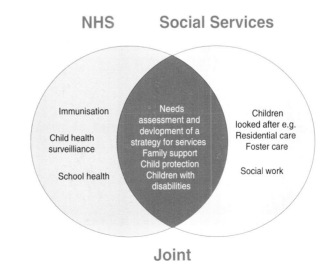

Source: Audit Commission

Exhibit 3
COMMUNITY HEALTH AND SOCIAL SERVICES EXPENDITURE ON CHILDREN
Services cost approximately £2 billion a year

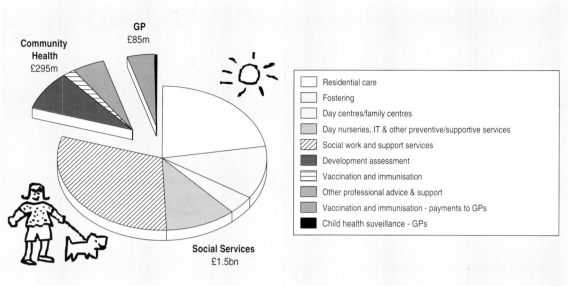

GP
£85m

Community Health
£295m

Residential care
Fostering
Day centres/family centres
Day nurseries, IT & other preventive/supportive services
Social work and support services
Development assessment
Vaccination and immunisation
Other professional advice & support
Vaccination and immunisation - payments to GPs
Child health surveillance - GPs

Social Services
£1.5bn

Source: CIPFA PSS statistics 1991/2, DH FR22 Returns 1991/2, FHSA Annual Accounts 1991/2, Welsh office

surveillance – mostly undertaken by health visitors working in the GP practice. In the two years following the introduction of the new contract the proportion of children on accredited GPs' lists had risen from 30% to 50% of the child population. More recent estimates by the British Medical Association (BMA) suggest that this figure is now nearer 60% (Ref. 8).

8. Social services in England and Wales spend about £930 million on direct services such as residential, fostering and day care for children, and about £570 million on social work and indirect services.

9. In order to ensure that these very considerable resources are used to best effect, the Audit Commission has undertaken a study of current arrangements and how they are changing; and local auditors appointed by the Commission are reviewing arrangements in each health and local authority. The Commission is in an ideal position to help, as it audits both health and local authorities. Because of the scale and complexity of the topic, it has been necessary to limit the scope of the study: adoption services, services for

children with mental health problems, and for children and young people in trouble with the law have all been excluded. In due course they may be the subject of studies in their own right since the Commission acknowledges their importance to the well-being of children. The Commission also recognises the importance of education in a child's well-being. The Commission is particularly concerned about the rising numbers of children excluded from school. Hospital services for children who are sick have been covered in an earlier Audit Commission report (Ref. 9) as has education for children with special needs (Ref. 10). Voluntary sector organisations have a key role in providing services but their contribution has not been examined in detail. During the course of the study, eight local authorities and eight health authorities were visited and their services reviewed. Many other authorities were visited for more limited reviews of particular aspects of their services. This summary report is accompanied by a second document which provides more detailed evidence and guidelines for managers and practitioners.

The Key Themes

10. Both the Children Act and the NHS and Community Care Act place an emphasis on identifying people's needs and providing services to meet them. If identified needs are to be met, services must be effective. The Children Act also places an emphasis on providing these services in partnership with parents, supporting them in their child care role rather than taking over from them. The overlapping responsibilities of the agencies already outlined mean that these organisations must work together to provide a co-ordinated range of effective services.

11. To fulfil these expectations of the Children Act and the NHS Community Care Act the following key requirements are therefore necessary. Agencies must:

— focus on the needs of children and families and provide services which meet specific objectives relating to identified needs

— check outcomes to verify effectiveness of services

— work jointly to provide an integrated range of services and work in partnership with parents

To help the reader, the problems and solutions outlined below are identified by logos according to whether they represent:

— joint activity between the NHS and Social Services

— NHS activity

— Social Services activity

Problems Identified

12. At the time of Audit Commission visits to authorities progress towards these aims had been modest. Changes of such magnitutude must be managed carefully and cannot be implemented overnight. Authorities recognise these key themes and are aware of many of the challenges they face. Problems have been found with joint activity between health and social services, activity within the health service, and activity within local government. Each is considered in turn.

JOINT ACTIVITY

13. Despite common interests and overlapping responsibilities (Exhibit 2), collaboration between health and social services can be improved. Only a quarter of authorities visited had developed a joint approach to planning for children in need. Authorities seem unsure how to identify children in need as required by the Children Act, and few have agreed definitions, assessed the extent of need, set priorities or planned services together based on an assessment of needs.

14. **Family support** in particular is not being planned jointly. Apart from the mandatory joint reviews (with education) on services to children aged under eight, few authorities have an appreciation at strategic level that family support is a common area of interest and activity, especially since the increase in social services' responsibilities under the Children Act. This uncertainty is mirrored at practitioner level. At all authorities visited, there was some ambiguity in the roles of health visitors vis-a-vis some social services staff. This is in part because individual health visitors determine their own

roles and priorities in supporting families, without always being aware of the changing roles and activities of others. Record-keeping by health visitors should also be clearer. Management and other professionals involved with families do not know what needs health visitors have identified, or what actions they have taken with families and to what end. For their part, social workers have little spare time to organise support for families whose needs are not in crisis, and regard 'children in need' as a separate group with a low priority. Needless to say, given this background, outcomes are not often being measured – although in family centres in three social services authorities, programmes were being monitored against objectives.

15. Voluntary organisations play a major role in providing family support, from running family centres to providing volunteers to help parents with child care in the children's own homes. In authorities visited, however, there was a five-fold variation in the proportion of the budget spent by social services on this voluntary provision of family support. Not all authorities, for example, make use of such organisations as Homestart or Newpin which use parent volunteers to help support parents and children in need.

16. In contrast, collaboration between agencies over **child protection** arrangements is supported by considerable, firm procedural guidance from the Department of Health (Ref. 11). As a result, most authorities visited have taken steps to co-ordinate and clarify roles and procedures and work more in partnership with parents, although there are still some problems in getting good collaboration with schools and GPs. However, monitoring the activities in child protection is less well developed. For example in seven out of eight authorities visited, management information did not show the number of child protection referrals received and their progress through investigation recording for example, how many were dropped and why.

17. **Children with a disability**, in particular, need effective working arrangements between agencies providing services. Only one social services authority visited had yet reached an agreement with its corresponding health authority at a planning level. There are some good links among practitioners, but these depend on the individuals concerned and are therefore vulnerable to staff changes. Considerable friction between agencies – and confusion for parents – exists over the provision of special aids and equipment, and only two out of the eight authorities visited had resolved this issue. An Audit Commission survey of 131 families with a disabled child showed that only a quarter felt services to be well co-ordinated between agencies. In social services, the needs of children with a disability have a low priority because they are few in number.

* * *

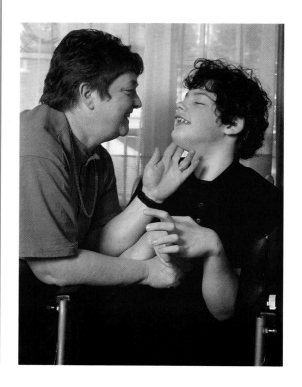

18. Although agencies should jointly agree much of the activity with children and families, each agency, individually, has functions which are primarily its own responsibility. Community child health services are considered first.

COMMUNITY CHILD HEALTH: IMMUNISATION, SURVEILLANCE AND SCHOOL HEALTH

19. Most commissioning health authorities visited have yet to assess the needs of their populations for community child health services (Exhibit 4). Some of these services will be those discussed in the previous section and the needs should therefore be decided jointly with others. Most authorities have policy statements on immunisation and child health surveillance which follow the Department of Health recommended programmes and targets (Refs. 12 and 13); and most have accepted the need to work more closely in partnership with parents, using parent-held health records which document immunisations and health surveillance checks among other things. But 'block' contracts are

still the norm, in which activity is specified based on crude indicators such as the number of face-to-face contacts made by health visitors.

20. **Immunisation** programmes have largely been successful. Targets are clear, there are good incentives and the work is often well co-ordinated. This may be due in part to GPs receiving additional payments where the proportion of children on their lists immunised exceeds certain thresholds. Many have achieved their targets.

21. In contrast, **child health surveillance** has yet to change significantly although commissioning authorities have generally set out their policies. Health visitors in authorities visited spent between 8% and 18% (with an average of 12%) of their time on such work (Exhibit 5, overleaf). But, in half of the community units and trusts visited, some health visitors were continuing to work to previous policies, conducting extra checks routinely without any evidence of extra need or extra benefit. Commissioning health authorities were generally unaware that health visitors were spending their time in this way.

Exhibit 4
ACTIVITIES OF HEALTH COMMISSIONING AUTHORITIES VISITED
They have yet to assess the needs of their populations

Authority	1	2	3	4	5	6	7	8
Strategic view	✓	✗	✓	✗	✓	✗	✗	✓
Needs assessment	✓	✗	✓	✗	✗	✗	✗	?
Contract specification	✗	✗	✗	✗	✗	✗	✗	✗
Inform./monitoring	✗	✗	?	✗	✗	?	✗	✗
Links with others	✓	✗	✓	✗	✓	?	?	✗
Quality assurance	?	✗	✗	?	?	✗	?	?

✓   Significant progress made by commissioners

?   Some progress made(but generally made by the provider or not disseminated)

✗   No significant progress made by the commissioners

Source: Audit Commission analysis of authorities visited

Exhibit 5

ACTIVITIES OF HEALTH VISITORS

Health visitors spent an average of 12% of their time on the programme of surveillance set down in policy

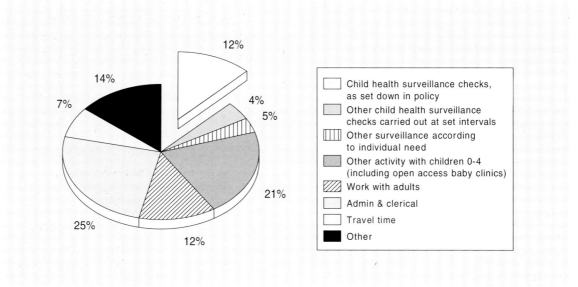

Child health surveillance checks, as set down in policy

Other child health surveillance checks carried out at set intervals

Other surveillance according to individual need

Other activity with children 0-4 (including open access baby clinics)

Work with adults

Admin & clerical

Travel time

Other

Source: Audit Commission analysis – authorities visited

22. Health visitors at community units and trusts visited also spent on average a further 20% of their time engaged in other activities with young children, including child health clinics. New mothers were sometimes being asked to attend regularly as a matter of course, regardless of individual need. Community child health clinics are in some cases also attended by clinical medical officers (CMOs) or senior clinical medical officers (SCMOs). With the growth of GPs accredited to undertake health surveillance, the need for such clinics should be reducing as should the routine involvement of CMOs. However, few authorities visited had a programme to reduce clinics – implying that scarce and expensive medical and health visiting resources were not being used to best effect and that provision was being duplicated unnecessarily.

23. Programmes of **school health** activity were under review in all authorities visited (although in only 9% of schools responding to an Audit Commission survey were head teachers also involved). There was a similar lack of clarity in this area. Services were

shifting toward a more specialist secondary role, whilst schools still saw services in a traditional way, focused on medical inspections and immunisations. Activities were not being targeted sufficiently, and full use was not being made of the skills of school nurses. Again, the role of CMOs was generally unclear.

24. Some of these problems have only recently come to light because information systems have generally been poor. Although computerised systems were in use in all health agencies visited, not all could provide information about their services in a useful form. Information on outcomes was even less readily available: for example, only one of the community trusts or units visited could tell, as a matter of course, how many children were correctly referred (with age of referral) for sensori-neural deafness – a usually congenital and irreversible condition which should be picked up by about eight months of age.

25. In conclusion, there appears to be a lack of clarity over service objectives and outcomes, with insufficient collaboration between professionals providing services.

SOCIAL SERVICES: SOCIAL WORK AND CHILDREN LOOKED AFTER AWAY FROM HOME

26. Although many areas of activity are shared by social services authorities with others, two key services remain their sole responsibility. These are social work and the care of children who are looked after away from home by social services departments (the new Children Act terminology for children 'in care').

27. Most social services authorities visited were in the process of developing new strategies for children's services – although usually without any preliminary assessment of children in need. Without such an assessment, strategies are likely to continue the current pattern of services in an uncritical way. Authorities' main challenge is to be able to release sufficient time and resources to tackle their wider responsibilities under the Children Act – but child protection work and work with children looked after continue to dominate both.

28. Field social workers in particular appear to have insufficient time to undertake more proactive work in support of children in need – particularly because of the pressures of child protection work. Recent research by Jane Gibbons et al (Ref. 14) on child protection referrals, investigations and registrations indicated that up to two thirds of referrals investigated were dropped before being considered for registration at a case conference. There was no suggestion that these referrals were dropped inappropriately, raising questions about the ways in which authorities respond to such referrals. Were criteria and risk indicators – if any – too imprecise to predict that a situation warranted registration rather than some other response? No other services were offered to a large minority of families where investigations were dropped. Quite apart from the trauma for the

families investigated, the drain on resources must be considerable.

29. Systems for managing the workload of field social workers were generally found to be inadequate. The caseload per social worker – usually the only workload measure available – does not adequately reflect activity as 'cases' can vary significantly in the amount of work required. However, only two authorities visited had introduced a workload management system with cases 'weighted' to reflect the work required. One of the authorities with such a scheme found that the workload varied widely between different social work teams (Exhibit 6) – suggesting a need for some reallocation of resources. The remaining authorities without such a system were not in a position to know how well their resources were being utilised or deployed.

30. **Children looked after** by the local authority (formerly known as children 'in care') use very considerable resources. Residential care is much the most expensive service available. Some placements can cost

Exhibit 6
FIELD SOCIAL WORK – WORKLOAD MANAGEMENT
Workload varied widely between different social work teams suggesting inefficiencies in the allocation of resources

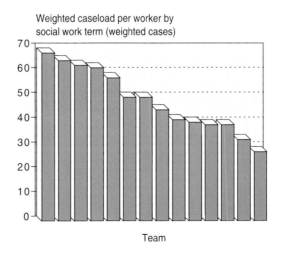

Source: Audit Commission analysis of data from a sample authority visited.

over £100,000 per annum. In 1991/92 the average weekly gross cost (excluding capital charges, overheads and social work) of a child in an ordinary English local authority community home was £659, compared with an average of £128 for a child in foster care (excluding the cost of foster care support – estimated to be about £25 per child per week). These averages mask a wide range of costs (Exhibit 7) which can, in turn, reflect a wide range of problems with different degrees of complexity.

31. Over the past decade, the pattern of care has been changing, reflecting the understanding that most children are better off with their own families, and that, apart from a small number of cases where residential care is the preferred option, most children away from home are better off in foster care. The number of children 'looked after' by local authorities in England has fallen from 95,000 in 1980 to 55,000 in 1992. The proportion of children in residential care has also declined markedly, from 29% in 1981 to 19% in 1992 although there is a wide variation between authorities in the proportion of children

'looked after' who are in residential care (Exhibit 8). The reasons for this variation have not been analysed in depth, but some authorities may still not be making full use of the major alternative, fostering. The percentage fostered varies between 40-78% of children looked after nationally, and 46% to 66% in the authorities visited. Two authorities visited considered that they could make further reductions to their residential care.

32. It is crucial that these resources are tightly managed. Looking after children away from home is not only expensive: research shows that outcomes (for example, educational achievement) for children looked after by social services authorities can be poor, especially where children suffer the further trauma of repeated moves because their placements in foster or residential care break down (Ref. 5). Practitioners should be able to pay more attention to these research findings which could help improve outcomes for children. The objectives in looking after a child away from home are frequently unclear; and assessments and individual care plans can

Exhibit 7
GROSS WEEKLY COSTS OF RESIDENTIAL AND FOSTER PLACEMENTS 1991/2
There are a wide range of costs, and complexity of children's problems...

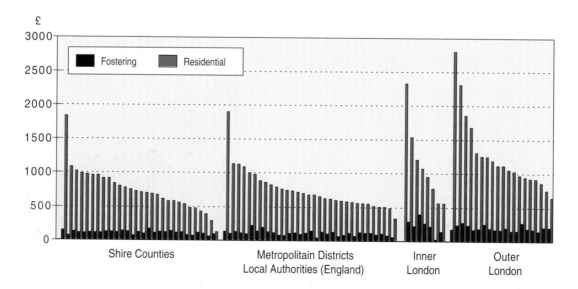

Source: Department of Health Key Indicators of Local Authority Social Services 1991/2.

SSD

Exhibit 8
PROPORTION OF CHILDREN LOOKED AFTER IN RESIDENTIAL CARE
...and a wide variation in the proportion of children 'looked after' who are in residential care

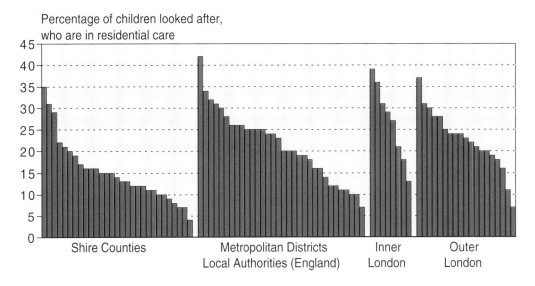

Percentage of children looked after,
who are in residential care

Shire Counties   Metropolitan Districts   Inner   Outer
                        Local Authorities (England)   London   London

Source: Department of Health Key Indicators of Local Authority Social Services 1991/2 (England).

be vague. In most authorities visited, guidelines for field social workers which could help to rectify this situation were generally lacking. Management information allowing the experiences of children 'looked after' to be monitored for risk indicators, such as breakdowns in foster or residential care, was not generally available, although in future the Department of Health will collect this information. Taking educational experience as an example, it was disturbing to note in the authorities visited, the number of children in residential homes who were not attending school (Exhibit 9). In three quarters of the authorities visited their situation was not being addressed sufficiently rigorously by social services and education departments working together.

33. Social services also have new responsibilities for young people leaving care at age 16+. Over half of authorities visited had set up a procedure for ensuring that a leaving care plan was prepared at age 14 or 15 but young people interviewed felt that field social workers lacked time to listen to them.

They felt that their social workers' skills were more appropriate for younger children.

34. **To Summarise,** authorities have yet to make the break from providing support dominated by a set range of services to an approach that is needs-led. There is insufficient collaboration or agreement

Exhibit 9
EDUCATION OF CHILDREN IN RESIDENTIAL HOMES
The number not attending school was disturbing

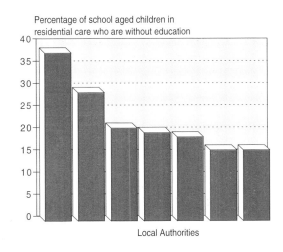

Percentage of school aged children in
residential care who are without education

Local Authorities

Source: Audit Commission analysis - authorities visited.

between agencies on defining and measuring the extent of children in need, setting priorities and planning services based on measurement of need. At practitioner level there is an ambiguity in the role of the health visitor vis-a-vis some social services staff. Community child health services lack sufficient clarity on priorities, objectives and outcomes and therefore cannot say how effective their services are in meeting needs. Contract specifications fail to make a connection between the amount of resources, the degree of needs and the cost of services. Meanwhile, social services authorities recognise that they remain locked into

protecting and looking after children and have problems fulfilling their broader responsibilities for children in need. Much greater attention must be given to identifying needs, and agencies must then work together and in partnership with parents to tackle them. Services must in future have clear objectives, and outcomes must be monitored against them. However, local government reorganisation is also of current concern to social services authorities as planning, co-ordination and inter-agency collaboration on services may well become more complex to arrange effectively and efficiently.

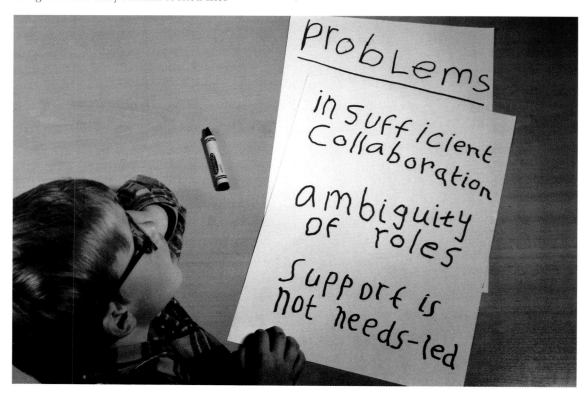

Joint

Moving Forward

35. Authorities and trusts need to address these issues both jointly and individually. The remainder of this report summarises what needs to be done, first by authorities working together and then individually.

WORKING IN PARTNERSHIP

36. Health and local authorities should, together, define what they mean by 'needs'. They must then, together, assess their extent and develop a joint children's strategy to address them (Exhibit 10). This strategy, set down in the Children's Service Plan, should be jointly published (with education) in the same way as community care plans.

37. Ideally this activity should be conducted in a multi-agency forum which should include housing agencies, education authorities, voluntary bodies and others. The Welsh Health Planning Forum has recently issued draft guidance to health authorities on working together (Ref. 15). It lists the five areas requiring joint action as defining needs, assessing their extent, prioritising between them, identifying the children concerned, and planning appropriate services. Experience so far suggests that total commitment from members and senior managers to a joint approach is crucial for success.

38. Assessing the extent of need is a new activity for most authorities but information is available to help them. Research studies have identified a number of indicators of need including poor housing, low income, and high prevalence of unsupported, young parents. Demographic data from the 1991 census, which includes such information, can be produced for individual electoral wards and can be particularly valuable in clarifying a

picture of where needs are likely to be high within a locality. Directors of public health have access to other valuable sources of information such as registers of children with a disability. Individual practitioners have detailed information on need at the local level, and in some cases this may be collated in practice profiles.

39. Many of these needs may be met by some form of **family support**. Family support

Exhibit 10
FIRST STEPS
Authorities should develop a joint children's strategy

> Define needs that should, or can, be addressed;

> Assess extent of these needs within the community;

> Decide what cost effective actions can be applied (there is little point in providing support that is not effective in ameliorating or alleviating a change;

> Decide with council members how needs are prioritised;

> Decide which statutory or other agencies should have, or share, responsibility and funding for services;

> Develop strategy and timetabled plans based on above;

> Monitor and evaluate outcomes;

> Record unmet needs and the reasons that they are unmet;

> Decide which, and how, polices are to be reviewed.

Source: Audit Commission

has yet to be widely recognised as a service requiring joint planning and co-ordination, although practitioners locally often recognise their inter-dependence (with health visitors described as the 'eyes and ears' of social services departments, for example). The amount and type of family support required depends on the findings of needs reviews. Authorities must think carefully about priorities, and then work out who is going to do what. For example, while all families with a new baby should receive an initial visit from the health visitor, thereafter health visiting should be based on clearly stated priorities and criteria. The assessed needs of individual families, the action taken and resulting outcomes should be clearly documented in accordance with published health visiting standards. Almost inevitably, there will need to be some adjustment to the number and types of staff required, and resources may need to be distributed differently between priorities and across localities. The involvement of voluntary organisations in family support will be important.

40. In social services, there should also be some rebalancing in order to help family support services to develop. Traditionally, most child care cases have been channelled to social workers, who have acted as 'gatekeepers' for more specialised services (Exhibit 11). Following the Children Act, social services authorities have wider responsibilities for children in need – requiring the development of family support which at times may not necessarily involve social workers at all. This broader approach should allow the diversion of some families to other resources in the community that make use of a wider range of options (Exhibit 12) provided by voluntary bodies, health professionals and others, including social services and education authorities.

41. Such an approach requires a redirection of resources from the traditional

Exhibit 11

THE TRADITIONAL ROUTE FOR CHILDREN REFERRED TO SOCIAL SERVICES
Most child care cases have been channelled to social workers

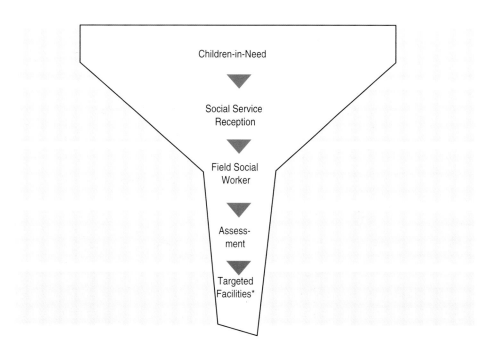

Note: * e.g. Social work, Children's homes, Foster parents, Family centres
Source: Audit Commission

Joint

areas of activity (A and B in Exhibit 12) to area C. In theory, effective investment in C should reduce the demand for A and B, reducing family stress and the need for crisis intervention; but in practice, such an effect has not yet been properly demonstrated and evaluated. Success no doubt also depends on good training, clear and well-understood procedures, effective assessments and clear individual care plans that are well managed and effectively monitored. It is important that diversion schemes are properly evaluated in a systematic way to ensure that they are effective in meeting the needs of children and families.

42. A successful strategy that diverts families away from potentially stigmatising, targeted, social services support depends on the development of an effective range of alternative services. Such a range should be developed in close co-operation with health, voluntary bodies and others, with closer working arrangements, shared facilities,

clearer working practices and joint funding of family support provided by voluntary bodies such as Newpin, Home-start, or community volunteers. Such voluntary family support provision should be available in all authorities.

43. Family centres could provide a suitable focus for much joint activity (Case Study 1, overleaf). Many are currently operated by social services departments or voluntary agencies and more are planned. They could, to advantage, become joint ventures between health, social services, education and voluntary organisations, providing a base for group work with families and children, child health clinics (other than those provided by GPs in their practices), peer support groups (in which parents support each other), nursery classes and playgroups, counselling and advice on housing and social security benefits and a base for staff making home visits. Placed in appropriate locations they could provide a 'one stop shop' for local communities.

Exhibit 12
A BROADER APPROACH
Allows the diversion of some families to other resources in the community

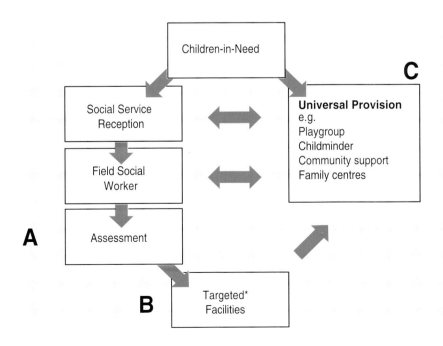

Note: * *e.g. Social work, Children's homes, Foster parents, Family centres*
Source: Audit Commission

Case Study 1
PEN GREEN CENTRE FOR UNDER 5S AND THEIR FAMILIES, CORBY

CLOSE CO-OPERATION WITH HEALTH AGENCIES AND OTHERS TO OFFER A VARIETY OF SUPPORT

Aims - Its aim is to offer a supportive environment, which will help children grow and develop. In some cases this will mean providing the child with stimulation through pre-school education or after school provision; in others it will mean providing parents with additional support in helping their children to develop.

Funding - joint, by Northamptonshire's Education and Social Services departments. Estimates for 1994 suggest a total LA contribution of £280,000. It also has close working relationships with the local health authority. Staffing is multi-disciplinary, with social workers, teachers, nursery nurses and health visitors involved with activities in the centre. There is a central role for parents themselves, in running some sessions. Much of the work crosses traditional professional boundaries.

Scale - scale of activity is difficult to estimate precisely given the range of activities. However a 'snapshot' suggests:

— Up to 300 adults may pass through the centre each day;

— 59 families use the nursery provision;

— 38 parents use drop-in facilities;

— 38 parents are involved in group work;

— 70 parents use the centre for other purposes.

Activities - various activities are on offer at the centre, both for families who have been referred by health or social services, and for families who simply wish to make use of the facilities on offer at the centre. Children with disabilities are integrated with children who are not disabled.

— *A nursery* - Pen Green offers a nursery where the curriculum has been developed jointly between social services and education. Half of the places are reserved for children or families who are felt to be in need. The remaining places are open, and are allocated on a first-come-first-served basis to children on a waiting list. However, the centre is sited in an area of high needs. There are 39 full time equivalent places, including a small number of places earmarked for children on the child protection register.

— *Play groups* - run by parents but facilitated by staff (25 places).

— *Support groups* - Staff offer some 25 support groups some of which will assist with parents suffering from stress or difficulty that resulted in a referral from the statutory agencies, and others that have been developed in response to the community's own expressed needs. In addition, parents run their own mutual support groups without the participation of staff, using the facilities of the centre, and the staff for advice and support if necessary. There is a crèche facility for parents using groups.

— *Drop in sessions* - There are also baby clinics, adult health advice sessions and other drop in sessions which are developed in response to local needs. Approximately 25 parents and children regularly use the drop in facility at any one time.

— *Outreach work* - staff undertake outreach work with families in their own homes on basis of individual need.

— *Other activities* - specific projects are funded separately and are developed in response to specific needs. These vary year on year and are not part of the 'core' activities of the centre.

44. Programmes of activity run by professionals and/or volunteers providing help, in a non-stigmatising way, to parents experiencing specific problems in bringing up their children can also be valuable (Case Study 2). The aims of such programmes are to help parents overcome problems with child care and to prevent the difficult behaviour exhibited by some children from deteriorating to the point of delinquency.

45. Although co-ordination and clearer procedures on **child protection** work are evident at authorities visited, better management information is required on activity. Systems are now available which monitor the level of referrals and how they are handled. This can be a valuable tool to help manage the workflow and check the appropriateness of the action taken. Where the lack of involvement by teachers is a problem, attention must be focused by social services and education departments on developing good liaison with school governors and head teachers.

46. One group in particular need of a higher profile are **children with a disability** and their families. Four key developments are required.

— First, the central role of parents should be supported with better information; GPs need to become more sensitive to the concerns expressed by parents.

— Second, parents need a 'one-stop-shop' such as the child development centre for young children where both health and social services can be accessed. There is no such obvious point of contact once children go to school, so alternative possibilities should be explored.

— Third, families who have a child with a disability whose needs are particularly complex should have a 'care manager' who co-ordinates the provision of services and helps families obtain the services they need.

— Fourth, health agencies, social services and education authorities, must develop effective ways of working together. There are some pilot schemes under way, and so far joint funding appears to be crucial to their success. Authorities can make a start in a modest but worthwhile way by introducing joint equipment budgets and joint respite care schemes – although such schemes must not be allowed to become too bureaucratic.

COMMUNITY CHILD HEALTH: IMMUNISATION, HEALTH SURVEILLANCE AND SCHOOL HEALTH

47. District health authorities must take stock of the current position on immunisation, surveillance and school health where this is not already known. Statistics on immunisation are more readily available than those on surveillance – partly because they are linked to payments to GPs and information to support payments is therefore collected. The coverage of the other universal services is usually less well known.

48. Once needs have been determined, a strategy for tackling them is required. Here, GPs – particularly fund-holders who purchase community nursing – should be involved as full and active participants at all levels of decision-making. FHSAs can encourage GPs to work within the agreed strategic framework by collecting useful information on the coverage and effectiveness of their activity, and providing GPs and primary care teams with feedback to assist in the development of services. Where GPs are accredited to conduct child health surveillance, FHSAs are best placed to monitor the quality of services and to feed back audit information. District health authorities have responsibilities for the health needs of the entire population; GPs' focus is more local. Health authorities will need to continue to commission additional 'public health' functions for local populations where services are otherwise provided by GPs working only with the families on their lists.

Case Study 2

SUPPORT TO PARENTS

OXFORD FAMILY NURTURING NETWORK

Aims

- To improve parenting skills and nurturing in families at risk of abusing and neglecting children. Aims to benefit both families with severe difficulties as well as those whose needs are less critical.

Method

- The project uses a formal process: 'The Nurturing Program of Parents and Children 4-12' developed in the USA combining parent education and nurturing with support from other parents.

- A maximum of ten families are taken through 15 weeks of two-and-a-half hour sessions.

- Children and parents, in separate groups, work on similar topics each week. For example:

  — child behaviour management that avoids violence

  — importance of praise

  — recognising feelings and personal needs.

  — assertiveness and learning to say 'no'

  — handling stress and anger

  — development stages of children

  — responsibility for own behaviour

  — drug and alcohol abuse

  — how to increase self esteem.

- Adults' group uses handbooks, video, discussion and role play.

- Children's group uses discussion, artwork, games, play-acting, puppets and music.

Staffing

- The project is run by three part-time co-ordinators: a clinical psychologist, health visitor and clinical nurse specialist.

- The co-ordinators train volunteers from the caring professions including teachers, social workers, health visitors and psychologists.

- Recruited and trained - 66 volunteers.

- Co-ordinators run the parents' group. Volunteers run the children's groups.

Set-up arrangements

- The network has charitable status and is Independent from health and social services it has charitable status, but collaborates with both

- Support procured from local health and social services authorities and approval secured from Area Child Protection Committee (ACPC).

Funding

- Joseph Rowntree Trust

NHS

- Funds also raised from social services, local charities, business and private donors.

- Funds also raised from social services, local charities, business and private donors.

Activity

- Each 15 week program is run from different social services family centres and other community centres.

- Referrals canvassed from social services, health visitors, primary schools, educational and paediatric psychology services and child psychiatric service.

- In 12 months 50 families have attended programmes. Most were one-parent families. Half of the fathers invited to participate have completed the course.

Evaluation so far

- Evaluation measures developed and piloted.

- American materials and approach are acceptable to participants, with parents reporting high levels of satisfaction.

- For those families who persevere with programme there are positive changes. Some families need more support before changes are sustained.

- Improvements in children's behaviour, and progress at school reported by some parents.

- Social services appreciative of positive changes in some client families.

- Evaluation of effect on families to be undertaken.

Budget (1 year)

- £85,000 to cover 3 co-ordinators, working three and a half days each per week, plus secretary, plus programme materials.

Future aims

- Lack of specific training noted among professionals (e.g. in primary care, schools and social services) on how to manage difficult behaviour shown by children. Aim to develop training in the project's methods nationally.

49. Contracts with providers of community child health services should then specify the **immunisation** and **child health surveillance** programmes required (which would usually be in accordance with the recommendations of the Department of Health). Contracts should also specify the core programme of health visiting activity, over and above a single, universal visit for families with a new baby. Some of this activity should be the result of joint strategies for children in need and clarified roles and responsibilities for family support as discussed earlier. Commissioning health authorities should review the provision of community child health clinics in the light of GP-based provision. They should start to move away from the existing unspecific 'block' contracts,

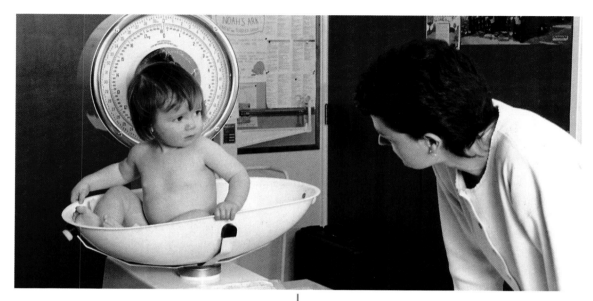

and specify the checks required, calculating the resources needed to deliver the resulting programmes. They should then monitor the extent of coverage and link contracts to the achievement of objectives. Actions by providers of community health services such as the appointment of 'co-ordinators' to take responsibility for programmes of surveillance on children's sight and hearing, monitoring coverage, effectiveness and referrals, will help to drive forward service improvements, and identify areas where further investment may be necessary.

50. **School health services** also need more direction. Many aim to become more focused, moving away from medical examinations for all pupils regardless of need, towards a more specialist service providing support for disabled children, health promotion, sex education and other such activities. Some school nurses will need additional training as counselling and the provision of health promotion and education are skilled tasks. Once again, the service should be based on needs with agreed objectives and monitored results. Some authorities are beginning to address these issues (Case Study 3). In recognition of the changing role of the school health service, the BPA has produced a discussion document to further this debate (Ref. 16).

51. Similarly, the role of clinical medical officers is changing. Many have acquired considerable experience in community child health without necessarily obtaining formal qualifications. Recognising this, a recent report (Ref. 8) recommended that the medical officer grades should be integrated into the mainstream medical career structure within a combined child health service. The BMA envisages that more of the medical input to community child health should be delivered by doctors in the training grades, although with a continuing need for some career grade posts below consultant to give some continuity of medical staff in the community. Duties appropriate to the career grade doctors include the provision of support to social services in fostering and adoption work and to education in the preparation of statements of special needs.

52. Underpinning all of this should be much better management information. As a result of a systematic approach to child health surveillance and simple, but effective information systems, research over six years in Northumberland has shown significant improvements in the processes and outcomes in this area of activity (Case Study 4). Immunisation co-ordinators have been particularly successful in monitoring progress, and similar co-ordinators should be identified

Case Study 3

SOME AUTHORITIES ARE ADDRESSING THE ISSUES

SCHOOL HEALTH REVIEW IN RIVERSIDE COMMUNITY HEALTH CARE NHS
TRUST

The school health service was reviewed to examine cost-effectiveness in the context of population needs (ethnic composition, homelessness, children on the child protection register, and local anecdotal information about prevalence of substance abuse, such as glue sniffing, and expulsions from school). The services changes proposed could be accommodated within existing resources. The results were:

General

— To promote the CMO and School nurse (SN) as a school health team with common management. SNs with further training to supervise and support others, identify health needs, set targets and prioritise work.

— Explicit contracts to be established between the School Health Service and each school consisting of a core programme for all schools, and additional services targeted to local needs.

— Training targets set for SNs.

— A commitment to improve communication with GPs - GPs to be notified of all referrals.

Immunisation

— An expanded role of the SN in opportunistic immunisation.

Health promotion

— Evaluation via knowledge and attitude surveys before and after health promotion sessions.

— With the agreement of schools, health promotion sessions to be incorporated into curriculum, following the Health of the Nation priorities and National Curriculum targets.

— Regular open health sessions in secondary schools to be considered (and firm objectives set).

— A sexual health team to continue to visit schools.

Surveillance

— Medical examinations of all children starting school replaced by selective examinations following assessment by SN.

— Termly returns monitoring activity, immunisation uptake and crude outcomes to be made by school health team.

Child protection

— A health plan to be developed for all children on the child protection register.

— CMOs and SNs to attend case conferences. If CMO is unable to attend a written report to be sent.

— A commitment to maintain child protection training, and to develop audit during the following year.

Children with special needs

— Termly return to identify prevalence of children with special needs and improve targeting.

Case Study 4

EVALUATION OF THE HEALTH SURVEILLANCE OF PRE-SCHOOL CHILDREN IN NORTHUMBERLAND

SIGNIFICANT IMPROVEMENTS HAVE BEEN
ACHIEVED

- The immunisation cover for measles has risen from 58% to 96%, for diphtheria, tetanus, and for polio from 78% to 97% and for pertussis from 30% to 91%.

- The screening test cover has risen for 6 week tests from 79% to 96%, for 8 month tests from 80% to 90% and for 3 year tests from 79% to 88%.

- The median age at which deafness greater than 60 decibels is recognised has fallen from 18 to 9 months. The proportion of deaf children recognised after age 12 months has fallen from 55% to 37%.

- The median age at which cerebral palsy is recognised has fallen from 7 to 4 months for quadriplegia and from 9.5 to 7 months for hemiplegia. The upper quartile age has fallen from 10 to 7 months for quadriplegia and from 25 to 10 months for hemiplegia.

- The median age at referral for speech therapy for language disorder needing special educational provision has fallen from 40 to 28 months. The proportion of such children recognised after age 3 years has fallen from 56% to 16%.

- The proportion of boys undergoing orchidopexy for cryptorchidism before age 6 years has risen from 18% to 42%. [An operation to fix the testis in the scrotum, done in certain cases of undescended testis].

Source: Dr Allan Colver

for health surveillance, in particular to monitor hearing and sight checks. They should be responsible for ensuring maximum coverage at the appropriate age. They should also ensure that tests are conducted as effectively and efficiently as possible and that subsequent action is taken appropriately. Information on the results of such activities should be required by commissioning health authorities. Information on workloads for professional staff should be gathered to enable resources to be targeted at areas of greatest need (Case Study 5).

SOCIAL SERVICES: SOCIAL WORK AND CHILDREN LOOKED AFTER AWAY FROM HOME

53. Following broad assessments of need which should be conducted jointly as described earlier, social services authorities should review their current service patterns, to see how well they match needs. Indeed, most authorities visited had reviewed, or were reviewing, elements of their services. A thorough review of social work should be included in any examination of services. If they are then to discharge their wider responsibilities under the Children Act, they will need to divert resources away from traditional areas of expenditure (Exhibit 12).

Case Study 5

HEALTH VISITING IN NOTTINGHAM COMMUNITY HEALTH NHS TRUST

RESOURCES WERE TARGETED TO NEEDS

— Objective categories of need have been agreed by health visitor managers.

— All cases held by health visitors are classified according to category of 'need'.

— Cases are then deemed in need of 'high', 'medium' or 'low' levels of intervention.

— Classification of cases and the subsequent interventions by health visitors are reviewed with practitioners and managers, for appropriateness.

— Information from this system is used by managers to switch resources between localities, to match resources to needs.

— Traditional 'case-count' methods of workload management are not used.

54. Field social workers spend much of their time on **child protection** work, as already described, but much investigation work is dropped as inappropriate. It ought to be possible to tighten and clarify the guidelines and risk indicators that trigger a full child protection investigation. Improvements need to be carefully designed, however, and firmly rooted in research wherever possible, in order to ensure that genuine problems are picked up. This suggests that guidance on risk management should be given nationally by the Department of Health and the Welsh Office and further consideration by them given to the future direction of child protection services. The productivity gains which should eventually follow from better focusing could free resources for social workers to specialise in other activities - for example, in family support, work with adolescents or children with disabilities.

55. Similarly, the inadequacies of workload management systems have been described earlier. It is important that field social workers' caseloads should be well managed to ensure that proper attention is being given to priorities, that social workers have a fair workload (neither too little nor too much), and that resources are being matched to need across localities. A workload management system should be introduced which:

— is consistent throughout the department

— sets priorities

— takes account of workers' experience

— provides good information to managers

— provides aggregate information to senior managers

56. In addition to a formal workload management system, authorities should also have a method for monitoring quality. There are various possible approaches. For example, there is an assessment tool for children 'looked after' recommended by the Department of Health (Ref. 17) which can be used to review the quality of the work done. During supervision, team leaders (and occasionally more senior managers) can undertake thorough case reviews to assess the quality of the social work, sometimes accompanying social workers on selected

visits. Peer reviews – similar to clinical audit - can also be undertaken.

57. As with community child health services, activities should be underpinned by effective information systems. Traditionally, systems have recorded service activity. Detailed information has rarely been available about children's experiences of services – further reflecting a service-driven approach. Under a needs-led approach, systems should focus increasingly on the needs of children and families. They should record such indicators as the number of changes of address a child has while being looked after, the number of times a child is accommodated by social services, the objective and outcome of such care and the numbers referred for child protection. Such information is essential if quality is to be monitored and workloads managed effectively.

58. **Children looked after** by local authorities consume a very considerable amount of resource each year and it is essential that this resource should be tightly managed. Fostering and residential care should be seen as part of a spectrum of support, meeting different needs in different ways. Residential care should not be regarded as an option of last resort when all else fails. It should have a clearly defined purpose and

ethos offering specific support for specific needs. Each residential home and each fostering scheme should be clear about its aims and particular 'niche', and have a clear understanding of what it is aiming to achieve with the children and young people it is looking after. Residential care staff also have skills to offer in helping to assess children for services such as residential and foster care.

59. An effective fostering scheme should have a number of key features (Box 1). Good support and training for foster carers is essential. Their absence appears to affect the recruitment, retention and quality of foster carers more than any other factor (including levels of payment). Authorities wishing to reduce residential care further should strengthen foster support first. One fostering officer should not be expected to support more than twenty carers (counting couples as one) – the average number in the authorities visited where fostering schemes had the key features described in Box 1. For highly specialised schemes, such as remand fostering, this number may need to be even lower.

60. Residential care needs to be resourced and managed appropriately. Staffing levels should be sufficient for the tasks in hand. According to the report on the Staffordshire 'pindown' enquiry, no member of staff, no

SSD

Box 1

IMPORTANT ELEMENTS OF A FOSTERING SERVICE (as illustrated by Coventry City Council)

— A specialist fostering team.

— Regular information on the precise needs of children requiring placements.

— A recruitment process geared to precise needs (if necessary, on those of individual children).

— An agreement on the aims and outcomes of a placement (set out in a care plan).

— Monitoring of outcomes and changing needs.

— Support and training of foster carers to equip them for their tasks.

— A central point from which information on foster care vacancies and their characteristics can be obtained by social workers.

Source: Audit Commission

matter how well qualified or experienced, should be on duty alone with children (Ref. 18). A minimum of eight or nine staff are likely to be required for even the smallest home with the easiest tasks – hence the high costs illustrated at exhibit 7, which are further increased if occupancy rates are low. With a higher proportion of children or young people in residential care with a greater range of problems, staff numbers are likely to be even higher. Where school attendance is low (Exhibit 9), more staff may be required during the day while education and social services authorities find a long term solution to this problem. Given this sort of investment, it is very important that residential care is used appropriately, with clear aims and objectives, clear referral criteria, thorough assessments and care planning, and regular monitoring of progress (Box 2). The importance of these issues is well recognised, and a government-initiated support force is currently examining them in detail and advising authorities accordingly.

61. Specialist support from psychologists for foster carers and staff in homes can be of benefit in helping them to work with the challenges presented by the children and young people in their care. One social services department has appointed two psychologists to provide this kind of support. The psychologists are currently evaluating their work and early indications suggest that staff and foster carers find it of great value.

62. Social services and education need to accept joint ownership of the problem of disrupted education of children 'looked after', and work together to find solutions. At one authority visited, the social services department has appointed a qualified teacher as an 'education liaison officer'. An essential element of her role is to establish good relations with schools to create a co-operative approach in which problems with children can be tackled effectively. She also co-ordinates community-based activities for children or young people including youth projects and the Community Services Volunteers. She offers support and encouragement to the children and young people, for instance by trying to ensure that the right environment exists for homework. During 1991/92, she supported 34 children, of whom only two were permanently excluded from school following her intervention. This illustration provides just one model for

Box 2

IMPORTANT ELEMENTS OF A RESIDENTIAL SERVICE (as illustrated by, and quoted from The Strategy For Challenging Behaviour – South Glamorgan County Council).

- Principles/Standards underpinning the Strategy are written down.

- General aims and detailed objectives are set out in written guidance, e.g.

  — 'to work constructively with children aged 10 to 16 who display seriously challenging behaviour';

  — 'to ensure all alternative plans have been explored before removing a child from home';

  — 'to reduce or eliminate presenting behaviour problems'.

- Criteria are laid down for referral to the scheme. (These were decided after reference to research and government guidelines.) Criteria cover:

  — unsocialised behaviour

  — aggression and violence

  — inappropriate sexual behaviour

  — self abuse

  — substance abuse

  — firesetting
  (to assist potential referers a checklist is provided for each criterion)

- Referral route is set out in guidelines, together with form of assessment and who should do it (joint between referring agency/social services team, member of appropriate team operating the strategy and the family), and the time scale for completion.

- Procedure is laid down in guidelines for a planning meeting to consider the assessment and the consequent objectives. Responsibility for chairing and minuting meeting also set out. Objectives include e.g.

  — to accept/reject referral

  — to establish/review care plan

  — to match child's needs to resources

  — to make agreements with family

  — to allocate case accountability

  — to identify how/when plans will be reviewed

- Once child placed in home his/her progress against objectives of care plan is reviewed weekly with child.

- Placements are formally reviewed monthly to prevent 'drift'.

- Each home has a stated purpose and written procedural guidelines.

- Management structure and responsibilities are laid down.

- Support structure in place, including: 24 hours community resource team to undertake assessments, support families and develop community resources; and an education liaison officer to facilitate a child's educational placement.

tackling the difficult problem of disrupted education for children 'looked after'.

63. A leaving care policy should have two stages: preparing a young person before they leave foster or residential care; and helping them to adjust to independence or a return to their families once they have left. Preparing a young person for leaving care requires:

— a method for developing a leaving care plan for the young person at the age of 14 or 15;

— clear responsibilities as to who is to co-ordinate the plan.

In addition, there should be a formal monitoring system to ensure these processes take place effectively.

64. Having left care, young people need additional support in order to learn to cope with being alone and to take responsibility for their own lives. It has been found to be useful to appoint somebody to support and keep in touch with young people who have left care. Those who have left care may reject a traditional view of social work – at least in the short term. One young person commented that it was easier to relate to someone 'who's not like a social worker'.

*   *   *

65. Health commissioners, providers and social services must recognise the resource and time requirements implied by these proposals. But the gains in efficiency and effectiveness as services are focused more precisely on needs should more than off-set any additional investment.

66. All of these proposals require co-ordinated action if they are to be implemented successfully. Each agency will need to set out an action plan: an outline summarising the key points is set out overleaf.

ACTION PLAN

Central Government should consider:

- raising the status of joint children's services plans by making them obligatory and requiring publication;
- providing guidance to social services on risk management and criteria for child protection investigations;
- commissioning further research into effective family support measures.

Joint action between health, social services and education authorities should be set out in **children's service plans.**

Authorities should:

- agree detailed definitions for children in need
- assess the extent of these needs and agree priorities
- decide on effective ways of addressing these needs
- cost the service implications, and agree responsibilities and funding
- develop a strategy and set out plans with clear timetables
- monitor progress and evaluate outcomes, adjusting the strategy as necessary.

Services requiring a joint approach include family support, child protection and services for children with a disability:

Family support should be co-ordinated

- the role and activities of health visitor should be evaluated and co-ordinated with social services staff undertaking similar activities
- family centres should be developed as a suitable focus for family support work, with support given to voluntary sector schemes

Child protection needs greater co-ordination:

- closer working between health visitors and social workers should be encouraged, possibly through specialist health visitors attached to child protection teams who can support and advise colleagues
- area child protection committees could provide a framework for co-ordination.

Children with disabilities require four initiatives to be taken jointly by authorities

- the central role of parents must be supported, with good information and helplines
- a single point of reference should be provided through which parents can access both health and social services
- a single person should co-ordinate care for an individual child and family
- joint policies, strategies and operational arrangements should be developed.

Within this joint framework **health commissioners** must work with **providers of community child health services** to shape and direct health services more effectively. They should together insure that:

- immunisation and child health surveillance programmes are carried out in accordance with national guidelines
- initial visits are made by health visitors to all new babies but subsequent visits are only made to families with assessed needs
- written information is provided to parents, supported by a helpline
- child health clinics are provided to meet needs, and reduced where GP practices are providing alternative clinics
- the school health service's role is defined and refocused
- information systems and evaluation techniques are developed

providers of services will also need to ensure that:

- the skill mix of staff matches the workload.

Within this joint framework **social services** must develop a pro-active rather than a re-active approach to fulfil their responsibilities to children in need. They should ensure that:

- existing services and costs - including field social work practice and organisation - are reviewed
- wherever possible, resources are released to allow more pro-active interventions. In particular:-social work is focused more carefully, (with better screening of time consuming child protection referrals for example) and better directed through a caseload management system -services for children looked after have a clear focus, with effective support for foster carers and proper leaving care strategy
- 'diversion' strategies are promoted that invest in preventive work
- information systems are improved, to link needs, service activity and outcomes.

Annex 1

Thanks are due for the advice and guidance of the following who were members of the external advisory group to the project.

John Butler	Professor, Centre for Health Service Studies, University of Kent at Canterbury
Allan Colver	Consultant Community Paediatrician, Northumberland DHA
Carolyn Hey	Deputy Chief Inspector, Social Services Inspectorate, Department of Health
Roy Parker	Professor of Social Policy and Planning, University of Bristol
Chris Perry	Director of Social Services, South Glamorgan County Council
John Rea Price	Director, National Children's Bureau
Ron Spencer	Chief Executive, Cornwall DHA and FHSA
Sheila Shribman	Consultant Community Paediatrician, Northampton General Hospital
Barbara Stilwell	Lecturer, Institute of Advanced Nurse Education, Royal College of Nursing
Norman Tutt	Social Information Systems (former Director of Social Services, Leeds City Council)
Ian White	Director of Social Services, Oxfordshire County Council

*   *   *

Special thanks are also due to:

David Hall, Professor of Community Paediatrics, Sheffield Children's Hospital who gave the project team considerable extra advice and guidance in the preparation of the report and the audit guide; and Dr Barry McCormick, Director of the Children's Hearing Assessment Centre, General Hospital Nottingham who gave additional advice to the project team on hearing impairment in young children.

Under the directorship of Dr Ross Tristem, assisted by David Browning, the project was undertaken by Claire Blackman and Beverley Fitzsimons. Jonathan Sercombe and John Russell assisted in the preparation and analysis of data. Full-time assistance was given by Colin Bott, Social Services Inspectorate, Department of Health and Jean Georgeson, former director of community nursing. Consultants to the team were Rob Sykes, Director of Operations, Oxfordshire social services and Anthony Harrison. The Artwork was inspired by Laura Sykes (Aged 5).

SSD

Appendix 1

DIAGNOSTIC - SOCIAL SERVICES

STRATEGIC DIRECTION

Does the Authority have a clear, written strategic direction for services for children

— developed in collaboration with and agreed by other agencies, the public and the voluntary sector;

— reflecting the philosophy of the Children Act, to promote well-being as well as prevent harm?

Is this backed up by clear, timetabled objectives for service development, again in collaboration with other relevant agencies and reflecting the need to promote well-being as well as protect and provide accommodation for children?

NEEDS BASED APPROACH

Does the Authority have a needs-led rather than service-driven culture with individual workers having the capacity to package services in relation to need?

Is the Authority responding to the Children Act's drive to promote well-being, especially for children in need?

Has the Authority 'assessed the extent to which there are children in need in their area', preferably in collaboration with other agencies and interested parties to identify geographical areas of high need to aid with location of services?

Has the Authority established a local interpretation of children in need, to support practitioners in the delivery of services, in accordance with the Authority's strategic direction?

APPROPRIATE INFORMATION AT SENIOR MANAGEMENT LEVEL

Do senior managers routinely receive information on key activities of the department which enables them to assess important quality issues? For example,

On child protection:

— delays in statutory processes

— unallocated cases

— variations in practice between teams

For children 'looked after':

— numbers looked after, by age, sex, reason and accommodation

— use of emergency placements

— use and cost of placements in the independent sector

MANAGEMENT ARRANGEMENTS THAT SUPPORT THE STRATEGIC DIRECTION

Do the management arrangements reflect the philosophy of the Children Act, to promote well-being as well as protecting children from harm:

— With specialised workers in areas that may otherwise receive low priority - such as specialist workers for children with disabilities;

— With a mechanism that monitors workloads for field workers;

— With built-in flexibility that allows workers to put together packages of services in relation to individual needs of children and families.

POLICY IN PRACTICE

Under 8s / family support services

— Is the authority's commitment to promoting well-being supported by the provision of a range of services for under 8s that is likely to reflect the range of needs that might exist - for example, including community based peer support groups?

— Has the Authority published the inter-agency review of under 8s services, which was undertaken in collaboration with the health authority, which sets out the agenda for future servic developments in relation to needs?

— Is the Department clear about the concept of family centres, their nature and purpose, and the extent to which they will be developed?

Children looked after
— Does the pattern of use of residential and foster care accord with the authority's strategic objectives?

— Is the authority achieving high rates of foster care use (approaching 70% of children looked after)?

NUMBER OF CHILDREN IN FOSTER CARE AS A PROPORTION OF ALL CHILDREN LOOKED AFTER (1991/2)

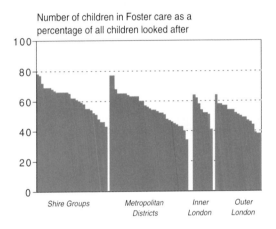

Number of children in Foster care as a percentage of all children looked after

Source: *Key Indicators of LA Social Services. (England 1991/2). LAs grouped according to similar characteristics*

— Are attempts being made to improve opportunities for successful fostering (such as adequate support for foster carers; adequate provision for information to foster carers when establishing foster placements; special fostering schemes)?

— Are senior managers aware of the adequacy of educational provision for young people who are 'looked after' by the Authority? Does the authority know how many children looked after are not regularly attending school?

— Is the authority aware of its relative position in terms of unit costs for the

residential provision it uses. Can it explain the variation?

GROSS EXPENDITURE ON CHILDREN'S RESIDENTIAL CARE (ALL SECTORS) PER CHILD PER WEEK (1991/2)

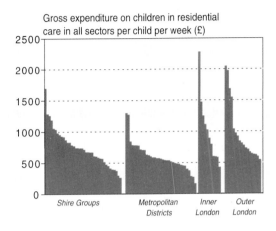

Gross expenditure on children in residential care in all sectors per child per week (£)

Source: *Key Indicators of LA Social Services. (England 1991/92). LAs grouped according to similar characteristics*

Leaving care
— Is there a systematic process by which young people 'looked after' by local authorities are 'prepared' for the transition to independence?

— Does the Authority have a policy which sets down its intentions to 'advise, assist and befriend' young people who have left 'care', which takes account of housing needs, health care needs and emotional support?

— Are there routinely collected indicators which demonstrate that this policy is carried out in practice?

Child protection
— Do ACPC reports clearly review child protection activity and set the agenda for future developments? Has the Authority responded to issues of concern to the ACPC?

— Are inter-agency procedures for child protection (revised since the Children Act) available to all practitioners working with children?

SSD

NHS

— Is adequate monitoring information available to senior managers (see above)?

Children with disabilities

— Is there an officer who is clearly responsible for policy and development of services for children with disabilities?

— Is there a process, streamlined across agencies, for the identification of children with disabilities, whose families may need help?

— Is the Authority certain that children with disabilities are treated as children first, with the same opportunities to make use of 'mainstream' children's services as any other children?

— Is there a register of children with disabilities, held either by health **or** social services, which acts as an aid for the planning of services across the district, and as a mechanism for co-ordinating services for individuals?

— Where duplicate registers must be held for boundary reasons, is relevant information shared as part of the needs assessment process, to aid service planning?

— Are there in place streamlined processes for agreeing funding and provision responsibilities for equipment for disabled children and respite care (which cuts across agencies)?

Appendix 2

DIAGNOSTIC - HEALTH COMMISSIONERS
STRATEGY AND POLICY

— Does the authority have a clear agenda for the health and well-being of children, with a strategy setting down how the health of the child population is to be improved?

— Does the authority have clear plans for children's community services, which reflect:

> — the need to link acute and community services;

> — the need to link medical, paramedical and nursing disciplines;

> — the need to reflect the activity of the primary care sector?

— Does the strategy include clear, resourced and timetabled plans for changes to service delivery?

— Is the strategy shared with other important agencies: the FHSA, GPs and Local Authorities, and developed in collaboration with health care providers?

NEEDS ASSESSMENT

— Is the strategy based on some assessment of the needs of the child population?

— Is there a shared view, with the local authority, of the concept of 'children in need' and are authorities working together to this common agenda?

— Is there any programme of review of the services currently being provided to asses the extent to which they meet the needs of the population?

COMMISSIONING PLANS AND CONTRACTS

— Do contracts set down:

> — comprehensive information on the nature and level of services, which go beyond traditional contact numbers;

> — some means of monitoring contracts meaningfully;

— specifications for the quality of services?

INFORMATION AND CONTRACT MONITORING

— Has the commissioner set down:

— Indicators of structure, process and, where possible, outcome which will indicate progress toward strategic objectives;

— indicators that are agreed in collaboration with providers, relying on a variety of data sources?

LIAISON WITH OTHERS

— Is the commissioner aware of its relative position in terms of staffing of community child health services? Can it explain the position?

HEALTH VISITORS PER 100,000 RESIDENT POPULATION (ENGLAND & WALES)

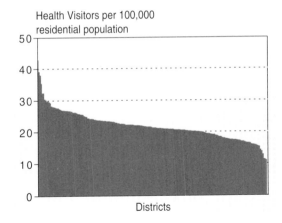

Health Visitors per 100,000 residential population

Source: Health Service Indicators 1990/91 and Welsh Office

— Has the commissioner developed its strategic approach in collaboration with other agencies, the voluntary sector and in consultation with the public?

— Are there arrangements in place at an operational level to ensure that services are delivered as seamlessly as possible? For example, in the provision and financing of equipment for children with disabilities. Is there a mechanism for monitoring this?

CMOS/SCMOS PER 100,000 RESIDENT POPULATION 15 (ENGLAND AND WALES)

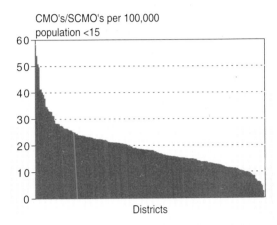

CMO's/SCMO's per 100,000 population <15

Note: * 20 districts have zero value

Source: Health Service Indicators 1990/1 and Welsh Office.

SCHOOL NURSES PER 10,000 SCHOOL POPULATION (ENGLAND)

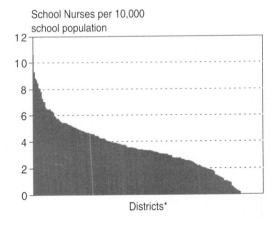

School Nurses per 10,000 school population

Source: Health Service Indicators 1990/91

Appendix 3

DIAGNOSTIC - PROVIDER UNITS

Strategic direction, needs assessment and information for contract monitoring are shared areas of responsibility with health authority commissioners. These should be developed in a collaborative framework, since providers are often in the key position to gather local level information on needs, service delivery and outcomes, to support the broader information that may be used by purchasers.

STRATEGY AND POLICY

— Does the authority have a clear agenda for the health and well-being of children, with a strategy setting down how the health of the child population is to be improved?

— Does the authority have clear plans for children's community services, which reflect:
  — the need to link acute and community services;

  — the need to link medical, paramedical and nursing disciplines;

  — the need to reflect the activity of the primary care sector?

— Does the strategy include clear, resourced and timetabled plans for changes to service delivery?

— Is the strategy shared with other important agencies: the FHSA, GPs and Local Authorities, and developed in collaboration with health care providers?

NEEDS ASSESSMENT

— Is the strategy based on some assessment of the needs of the child population?

— Is there a shared view, with the local authority and commissioner, of the concept of 'children in need' and are authorities working together to this common agenda?

— Is there any programme of review of the services currently being provided to asses the extent to which they meet the needs of the population?

INFORMATION AND MONITORING

— Does the provider unit supply:
  — Indicators of structure, process and, where possible, outcome which will indicate progress toward strategic objectives;

  — Indicators that are agreed in collaboration with commissioners, relying on a variety of data sources?

SERVICE DELIVERY - CORE SERVICES
Immunisation .

— Is agreed level of immunisation uptake (95%) being achieved across the district?

— Is there one person who is clearly designated as the immunisation co-ordinator, who is responsible for monitoring uptake across the district, for tackling local problems which are affecting uptake, and for providing advice to other professionals on immunisation matters?

Screening and child health surveillance

— Is the policy on pre-school child health surveillance in accordance with Department of Health guidance both in policy **and** in practice?

— Is coverage being achieved across the district, at the level agreed with the commissioners?

— Is there one person who is clearly designated as responsible for the surveillance programme, with responsibilities as described for immunisation co-ordinator (above)?

— Is the provider engaged in systematic clinical audit to examine the performance of the system, including monitoring ages at diagnosis for sensori-neural deafness and developmental delays?

— Are community units reconsidering their role in the light of greater GP involvement in this area?

Child protection
— Are there clear inter-agency procedures (revised since the Children Act) for dealing with suspicions of child abuse?

— Does the Unit have a clear training policy on child protection? (Does it audit its performance in achieving suggested standards of training for staff?)

— Are there designated facilities/approved practitioners for dealing with child abuse? (How successful is the unit in ensuring that all children who may have been abused are provided with these services?)

Children with disabilities
— Is there a process by which children with disabilities receive streamlined assessments of their needs, involving all relevant disciplines and fully involving parents? This should cut across agencies - with audit to ensure that this is being achieved in policy **and** in practice.

— Is there a register of children with disabilities, held either by health **or** social services, which acts as an aid for the planning of services across the district, and as a mechanism for co-ordinating services for individuals?

— Where duplicate registers must be held for boundary reasons, is relevant information shared as part of the needs assessment process, to aid service planning?

— Are there in place streamlined processes for agreeing funding and provision responsibilities for equipment for disabled children and respite care (which cuts across agencies)?

Health promotion and family support
— Do management processes for those staff principally involved in the delivery of health promotion work (health visitors and school nurses) ensure that health promotion activity reflects issues of concern in the district, and that a culture of evaluation is developed, to enable staff to focus on the most effective activities?

— Have senior management considered funding alternative methods of 'family support' – in discussion with local authority social services departments (for example, community-based peer support groups)?

Role and management of health visitors
— How do staffing and skill mix for health visiting compare with areas with similar levels of need?

— Can it be demonstrated that health visiting resources are distributed across the district according to need?

HEALTH VISITORS PER 100,000 RESIDENT POPULATION (ENGLAND AND WALES)

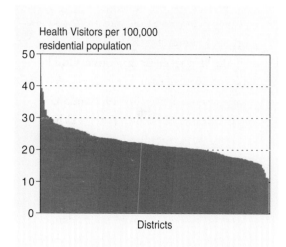

Source: Health Service Indicators and Welsh Office
          1990/91

— Do management processes for health
  visiting staff review the extent to which
  policies are carried out, and support staff in
  the development of services focusing on
  needs (e.g. meaningful caseload profiling;
  focusing home visiting where it is needed)?

Role and management of the school health
service
— How do staffing and skill mix for school
  health (as a whole) compare with other
  areas with similar levels of need?
(Skill mix should include the substitution of
nursing for some previously medical areas of
activity (e.g. immunisation, selection of
children for medicals on the basis of
interviews/pre-school records), to enable
medical aspects of school health to focus on
more specialist areas of expertise. Similarly,
there should be adequate clerical support for
medical and nursing staff).

— Have programmes of activity been
  reviewed in the light of current consensus
  (e.g. school entrant medical examinations)
  to enable resources to be freed up to focus
  on identified needs?
Service delivery - additional services over
and above the core programme of activity will

SCHOOL NURSES PER 10,000 SCHOOL POPULATION (ENGLAND)

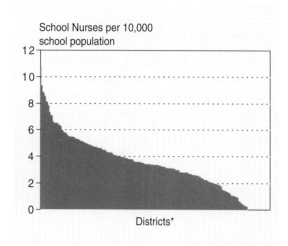

Source: Health Service Indicators and Welsh Office
          1990/91

CMOS/SCMOS PER 100,000 POPULATION 15 (ENGLAND AND WALES)

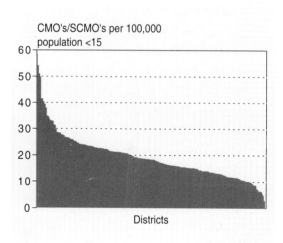

Source: Health Service Indicators and Welsh Office
          1990/91

be agreed in discussion with commissioners
and other agencies on the basis of need, and
with appropriate monitoring built in.

References

1. Children Act 1989, London HMSO.

2. Department of Health. General Practice in the NHS - 1990 Contract. 1989, London, HMSO.

3. NHS and Community Care Act 1990. London, HMSO.

4. Benzeval M and Judge K. Deprivation and poor health in childhood: prospects for prevention pp 291 to 324. In Otto H and Flösser G (eds) How to organise prevention - political, organisational and professional challenges to social services. 1992, Berlin, Walter de Giuytel.

5. Department of Health, Patterns and outcomes in child placements: messages from current research and their implications. 1991, London, HMSO.

6. Woodroffe C et al. Children, teenagers and health - the key data. 1993, Buckingham, Open University Press.

7. Office of Population Censuses and Surveys. The prevalence of disability among children. 1989, London, HMSO.

8. British Medical Association and NHS Management Executive. Report of the joint working party on medical services for children. November 1992. London, BMA.

9. Audit Commission, Children first: A Study of hospital services, 1993, London, HSMO.

10. Audit Commission, Getting in on the Act, Provision for Pupils with Special Educational Needs: the National Picture, 1992, London, HMSO.

11. Home Office, Department of Health, Department of Education and Science, Welsh Office. Working together under the Children Act 1989. 1991, London, HMSO.

12. Department of Health, Welsh Office, Scottish Home and Health Department, DHSS (Northern Ireland). Immunisation against infectious diseases. 1992, London, HMSO.

13. NHS Management Executive. Child health surveillance - a recommended core programme. HSG (92) 19, London, Department of Health. Also Welsh Office, Welsh Health Circular 92 (54).

14. Gibbons J et al, University of East Anglia. Unpublished research.

15. Welsh Health Planning Forum. Health and social gain for children: guidance to inform local strategies for health. August 1993, Cardiff.

16. British Paediatric Association. Health Services for School Age Children : consultation report of a joint working party. December 1993.

17. Parker R et al (eds). Assessing outcomes in child care: the report of an independent working party established by the Department of Health. 1991, London, HMSO.

18. Staffordshire County Council. The Pindown Experience and the Protection of Children: the report of the Staffordshire Childcare inquiry 1990. 1991, Staffordshire County Council.

Glossary of Terms

Accreditation   GPs for child health surveillance -FHSAs are required to 'accredit' as competent GPs who wish to receive additional payments under GMS for the provision of child health surveillance services.

Care managers   Person responsible for the co-ordination of services for an individual who has complex needs.

Care plans   Good child care suggests that all children for whom the social services department is providing specific services should have a child care plan which will describe the programme of services and intended outcomes desired from the services provided.

Child Development Centre (CDC)   A centre which brings together a multi-disciplinary team to assess the needs of and plan services for children with disabilities or other developmental problems.

Children's service plans   Documents to be produced by Social Services Departments, detailing plans for services for children.

Clinical Medical Officers (CMOs)   Career grade community doctors, who often have additional experience in child health.

Community Child Health Services (CCHS)   A wide range of health services , normally provided in the community, aimed to promote the health of children and protect them from disease. These services may be provided by acute or community units, or in a primary care setting by GPs, or by some combination of these.

Community Home   Children's residential home which may be run by the local authority, or the private or voluntary sector.

Developmental surveillance   Programme of checks or observations to ensure that a child is developing normally. Usually carried out by health visitors and either General Practitioners or Clinical Medical Officers for pre-school children.

Family centres   A number of models are available. The Children Act requires local authorities to provide family centres as part of their range of provision.They may be therapeutic, providing highly skilled interventions, or they may be a community-based/ self-help models of provision. Their unique feature is that they cater for children and families, unlike nursery or other day care provision.

Family Health Services Authorities (FHSAs)   Authorities which have responsibility for the commissioning and management of family health services. The commissioning role encompasses needs assessment and performance review: the provider role includes a wider responsibilkity for enhancing value for money infamily health services, as well as the pay and rations functions that were the remit of the predessor authorities - Family Practitioner Committees.

Family support   Any activity or facility provided either by statutory agencies or by community groups or individuals, aimed at providing advice and support to parents to help them in bringing up their children.

GP fundholders   General Practitioners who have elected to hold their own budgets for certain key elements of service.

Health Visitors   Nurses (who usually also have a midwifery training) who have undertaken a year's additional training to specialise in working in the community, with a broader public health / health promotion role. They nominally work with all client groups, although in practice the vast majority of their time is spent working with families who have children aged 0 to 5.

Homestart   A voluntary sector programme using volunteer mothers with some extra training to befriend other, vulnerable mothers to offer help and support.

Leaving care   Local authorities have increased responsibilities under the Children Act to provide advice and support to young people who have been in their care ('looked after') up to the age of 21 if necessary.

Looked after   Children Act term for children for whom the local authority is providing accomodation or care.

Need   Children in need terms formalised in the Children Act 1989 to include a child who is 'unlikely to achieve or maintain, or to have the opportunity of achieving or maintaining, a reasonable standard of health or development without the provision of services ... by the local authority; his health or development is likely to be sgnificantly impaired or further impaired without the provision for him of such services; or he is disabled'.

Newpin   A volunteer befriending scheme, intended to help support vulnerable or needy mothers, mainly through peer support but with some professional advice.

Parenting skills   Skills required by parents to enable them to bring up their children to a reasonable standard of health and development.

Peer support   The provision of help and support by individuals in the local community rather than by professional intervention.

Profiles   Community or caseload profiles produced by community nurses and GPs (health visitors and school nurses) to assist with the assessment of health needs in the community. They will include information on health status and mortality as well as broader

Public health functions In this context, the responsibility of community health staff, such as health visitors, to retain an oversight of the health needs of the community as a whole (e.g. accident rates, prevalence of health damaging lifestyles).

Register child protection Local Authorities are required to maintain registers of children who are at risk of 'significant harm'.

Respite care The provision of short breaks (either day care, foster care or residential care) for families of children (currently provided largely for children who have disabilities) where there may be high levels of stress.

School Health Service Services provided to ensure that the education of children is not jeopardised by poor health. These services may be provided by Clinical Medical Officers or General Practitioners, and School nurses. The school health service does not provide

indicators of health risks and services availability.

treatment services, but will offer health promotion, surveillance and immunisation, as well as more specialist functions such as supporting children with disabilities in school.

Sensori-neural hearing loss / deafness - hearing loss resulting from damage to the cochlear structures and nerve parts. They may be congenital or acquired.

Surveillance An unsolicited series of tests or observations designed to oversee physical growth and monitor development. The provision of child health surveillance also offers the opportunity to discuss broader health issues and concerns.

Workload management Systems developed in social services which classify the work (usually of social workers) into a number of broad categories with appropriate weightings for likely levels of effort required. Such systems provide important management information for social services managers.

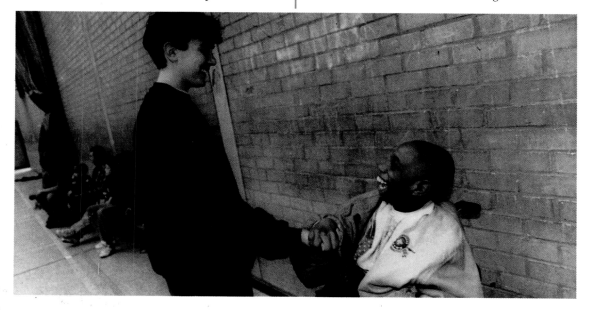

Seen But Not Heard

Co-ordinating Community
Child Health and Social
Services for Children in Need

LONDON: HMSO

© Crown copyright 1994
Applications for reproduction should be made to HMSO

Printed in the UK for the Audit Commission at Press on Printers, London
Photographs by Hilary Shedel, and Format Partners
Cover Photograph: with thanks to Hector and Hester
Illustrations by Nena Carney

ISBN 0 11 886125 5